The Poetry of Bliss Carman

Volume XVI - Rough Rider & Other Poems

William Bliss Carman was born in Fredericton, in New Brunswick on April 15th 1861. He was educated at Fredericton Collegiate School before moving to the University of New Brunswick, obtaining his B.A. there in 1881. As is common with so many writers his first published piece was for the University magazine and for Carman that was in 1879.

After several years editing various magazines and periodicals Carman first published a poetry volume in 1893 with Low Tide on Grand Pré. There was no Canadian company prepared to publish and when an American company did so it went bankrupt.

The following year was decidedly better. His partnership with the American poet Richard Hovey had given birth to Songs of Vagabondia. It was an immediate success.

That success prompted the Boston firm, Stone & Kimball, to reissue Low Tide on Grand Pré and to hire Carman as the editor of its literary journal, The Chapbook.

Carman brought out, in 1895, Behind the Arras, a somewhat more serious and philosophical work centered on the premise of a long meditation, using the speaker's house and its many rooms, as a symbol of life and the choices to be made.

In 1896 Carman met Mrs Mary Perry King, who rapidly became patron, adviser and sometime lover. She also became his writing collaborator on two verse dramas.

In 1897 Carman published Ballad of Lost Haven, and in 1898, By the Aurelian Wall, the title poem itself was an elegy to John Keats and the book was a collection of formal elegies.

As the century turned Carman was hard at work on a five-volume set of poetry "Pans Pipes". The excellence of a number of these poems did much to install Carman as the most noted of Canadian Poets and eventually their own Poet Laureate.

In 1912 the final work in the Vagabondia series was published. Richard Hovey had died in 1900 and so this last work was purely Carman's. It has a distinct elegiac tone as if remembering the past works themselves.

On October 28th, 1921 Carman was honored by the newly-formed Canadian Authors' Association where he was crowned Canada's Poet Laureate with a wreath of maple leaves.

William Bliss Carman died of a brain hemorrhage at the age of 68 in New Canaan on the 8th June, 1929.

Index of Contents

THE ANGELS OF MAN

The word of the Lord of the outer worlds
Went forth on the deeps of space,
That Michael, Gabriel, Rafael,
Should stand before his face,
The seraphs of his threefold will,
Each in his ordered place.

Brave Michael, the right hand of God,
Strong Gabriel, his voice,
Fair Rafael, his holy breath
That makes the world rejoice, —
Archangels of omnipotence,
Of knowledge, and of choice;

Michael, angel of loveliness
In all things that survive,
And Gabriel, whose part it is
To ponder and contrive,
And Rafael, who puts the heart
In every thing alive.
Came Rafael, the enraptured soul,

Stainless as wind or fire,

The urge within the flux of things,
The life that must aspire,
With whom is the beginning,
The worth, and the desire;

And Gabriel, the all-seeing mind,
Bringer of truth and light,
Who lays the courses of the stars
In their stupendous flight,
And calls the migrant flocks of spring
Across the purple night;

And Michael, the artificer
Of beauty, shape, and hue,
Lord of the forges of the sun,
The crucible of the dew,
And driver of the plowing rain
When the flowers are born anew.

Then said the Lord: "Ye shall account
For the ministry ye hold,
Since ye have been my sons to keep
My purpose from of old.
How fare the realms within your sway
To perfections still untold?"

Answered each as he had the word.
And a great silence fell
On all the listening hosts of heaven
To hear their captains tell, —
With the breath of the wind, the call of a bird,
And the cry of a mighty bell.

Then the Lord said: "The time is ripe
For finishing my plan,
And the accomplishment of that
For which all time began.
Therefore on you is laid the task
Of the fashioning of man;

"In your own likeness shall he be,
To triumph in the end.
I only give him Michael's strength
To guard him and defend,
With Gabriel to be his guide,
And Rafael his friend.

"Ye shall go forth upon the earth,

And make there Paradise,
And be the angels of that place
To make men glad and wise,
With loving-kindness in their hearts,
And knowledge in their eyes.

"And ye shall be man's counselors
That neither rest nor sleep,
To cheer the lonely, lift the frail,
And solace them that weep.
And ever on his wandering trail
Your watch-fires ye shall keep;

"Till in the far years he shall find
The country of his quest,
The empire of the open truth,
The vision of the best,
Foreseen by every mother saint
With her new-born on her breast."

THE ROUGH RIDER

There lift the peaks of purple,
Where dip the dusty trails,
Where gleaming, teeming cities
Lie linked by shining rails,
By shadow-haunted camp-fire,
Beneath the great white dome,
In saddle and in council
Intrepid and at home,

Who is the hardy figure
Of virile fighting strain,
With valor and conviction
In heart, and hand, and brain?
Sprung from our old ideals
To serve our later needs,
He is the modern Roundhead,
The man who rides and reads.

No pomp of braid and feathers,
No flash of burnished gear,
He wears the plainsman's outfit
Sufficient and severe.
With no imperial chevron
Upon his khaki sleeve,

He thinks by no made doctrine,
He speaks by no man's leave.

The breed and creed and schooling
Of Harvard and the plains,
Six hundred years of fighting
For freedom in his veins,
Let no one think to wheedle,
To buy, coerce, nor cheat,
The man who loves the open,
The man who knows the street.

He rides not for vain glory,
He fights not for low gain,
But that the range of freedom
Unravaged shall remain.
As plain as Bible language
And open as the day,
He challenges injustice,
And bids corruption stay.

Take up, who will, the challenge;
Stand pat on graft and greed;
Grow sleek on others' labor,
Surfeit on others' need;
Let paid and bloodless tricksters
Devise a legal way
Our common right and justice
"To sell, deny, delay."

Not yesterday nor lightly
We came to know that breed;
Our quarrel with that cunning
Is old as Runnymede.
We saw enfranchised insult
Deploy in kingly line,
When broke our sullen fury
On Rupert of the Rhine.

At Newbury and Worcester,
Edgehill and Marston Moor,
We got the stubborn courage
To dare and to endure.
From Ireton and Cromwell
We learned the sword and rein;
Free speech by truth made fearless,
From Hampden, Pym, and Vane.

A thousand years in peril,
By privilege oppressed,
With loss beyond requital,
Unflinching in our quest,
We sought and bought our freedom
And bore it oversea;
To keep it still unblighted,
We rode with Grant and Lee.

Now, masking raid and rapine
In debonair disguise,
The foe we thought defeated
Deludes our careless eyes,
Entrenched in law and largess
And the vested wrong of things,
Cloaking a fouler treason
Than any faithless king's.

He takes our life for wages,
He holds our land for rent,
He sweats our little children
To swell his cent per cent;
With secret grip and levy
On every crumb we eat,
He drives our sons to thieving,
Our daughters to the street.

He lightly sells his honor,
He boldly shames our pride,
And makes our cause a scandal
For the nations to deride.
So crafty, yet so craven!
One whisper through the mart
Can send him to his coffers
With panic in his heart.

With no such feeble rancor
As envy moves to hate,
No ignorant detraction
Of goodly things and great,
But with the wrath unbridled
Of patriots betrayed, —
Of workers duped by brokers,
Of brothers unafraid, —

Against the grim defenses
Where might and murrain hide,
Unswerving to the issue

Loose-reined and rough we ride
Full tardily, to rescue
Our heritage from wrong,
And stablish it on manhood,
A thousand times more strong.

Comes now the fearless Message,
The leader, and the time
For every man to muster
For honor or for crime.
Who would not ride beside him
Into the toughest fight —
For freedom, the republic,
And everlasting right!

THE SPIRIT IN ARMS

When the just ire of England
Arose in daring might
Against the perfidious Stuart,
To uphold a diviner right,
"Let kings learn," said her Commons,
"Their duty once for all,"
And sent the Lord's anointed
To the headsman of Whitehall.

But strange are the shifts for freedom,
Heavy tradition's hand,
And the days of the avenger
Were not long in the land.
No sooner another Stuart
Was safe on the throne once more,
Than his father's judges were outlawed,
Hunted from door to door.

Two oversea for safety
To wild New England fled,
To haunt her forest borders,
With a price upon each head.
Harried from hiding to hiding,
Eating their bread in haste,
By many' a hearth and camp-fire
Their unresting trail was traced.

To-day in sleepy Hadley,
In its wide, green-shaded street,

They will point you out a dwelling
Was the regicides' retreat.
Here between ranks of homesteads
Their public common was made
For pasture and pleasure, protected
From Indian pillage and raid.

Deep in the seeding grasses
The arching elm trees stand,
Under the blue of August,
With peace over all the land.
On such a day in summer
Seasons and seasons ago,
On this lovely Puritan haven
Descended the stealthy foe.

The people were all at worship,
When a sudden fiendish yell
Broke on the fast-day stillness;
They knew what it meant full well.
Forth rushed the men from the meeting
(Armed were they always then),
To find their quiet Main Street
Swarming with painted men.

Trapped, for the instant panic
Unmanning the stoutest there,
Drove them back to the doorway;
Disaster was in the air.
They saw their wives and children
Given to knife and brand,
And the blood ran back for a moment
From every hardy hand.

Mazed by the din and horror,
Stampeded by savage war,
Where was the spirit that triumphed
At Naseby and Dunbar?
Suddenly there before them,
Taking command, was seen
A thrilling resolute presence,
With heroic right in his mien.

At the call of that confident leader
Their sickened hearts grew bold,
And they thought how the Lord had smitten
The Midianites of old.
Then did the Puritan spirit

Come back to them where they stood,
And they fell on the shrieking Nipmucks
And drove them back to the wood.

But when the rout was over,
Ere the sweat was wiped away
From the tanned and toil-worn faces
In thankfulness that day,
They turned to behold the stranger
Who had saved them from worse than death,
And the spirit in arms had vanished,
He had come and gone like a breath.

Had they but looked on a vision?
Or, seeing them too sore tried,
Had the Lord sent His angel among them?
It was Goffe the regicide.
He had seen from his place of hiding
The redskins creeping down,
Malignant shapes in the shadows,
On the unoffending town.

And quick to the call of outrage,
He who could have no part
In the open life of his fellows
Had come to strengthen their heart.
The intrepid soldier of justice
Once more had unsheathed his sword
To defend the rights of a people,
Ere he passed to the great award.

THE PURITAN CAPTAIN

I saw in Newtowne lately a vision of the Spring, —
The glory of New England come back with blade and wing.
First came the sturdy willows, in coats of greenish grey
They marched beside the river in jubilant array;

And then along the roadsides where whitening orchards lean,
The pomp of golden hedges, with bannerings of green;
In deepest garden corners, bringing the wildwood near,
I saw the mystic trillium and the violet appear.

The far-off woodlands floated a mist of greyish blue,
With here and there the sanguine of maples showing through, —
The careless tinge of valor, the tatters of romance,

Inwoven in the habit of sober circumstance.

Through Craigie Street and Brattle the lilacs brushed the eaves,
Old gables stood transfigured in the miracle of leaves.
And where I passed at sundown under the twilight star,
Musing of those dead people who made us what we are,

From a colonial doorway, brass-knockered, prim and white,
Stepped forth a valiant figure, and in the uncertain light
Came down the sanded footpath with free imperious stride,
His classic cloak about him, his good sword at his side,

Uncompromising purpose in every move and line,
And in the clean-bred features a temper proud and fine.
His belted coat was homespun, his hat was steeple-crowned;
He walked and looked about him as one who makes a round.

A touch of old-world breeding both gracious and austere
In habit and deportment held me as he drew near.
"Good evening, Sir," he greeted the stranger passing by,
"It is a pleasant evening." "It is, indeed," said I.

At once his kindly manner had put me at my ease;
And as he stood there under the arch of lilac trees
Smiling at my amazement, I felt a kinship rise
To meet the thoughtful forehead, droll mouth, and fearless eyes.

My heart warmed of a sudden with deep ancestral fires.
Here were the very features and fervor of my sires.
He calmly spoke, this Pilgrim, half soldier, half divine,
Beneath whose grim demeanor I knew the soul benign.

"So God's eternal springtime comes back to earth once more,
His messenger of beauty to each New England door.
Rejoice ye in that message! I long ago but heard
Stern oracles of goodness, high callings of the word.

"I did not break Charles Stuart, to let the godless rule.
I did not raise up Cromwell, to tolerate the fool.
And I who fronted Andros the tyrant in Cornhill
And sent him back to cover, am with my people still.

Long, long I fought and suffered the blight of heinous things, —
The insolence of priesthoods, the arrogance of kings.
Against uncurbed oppression I drove with pike and sword;
And in the cry for justice I knew my spirit's Lord.

"I did not stop to quibble upon the path I chose.

When came the need for freedom, in freedom's name I rose,
To champion ideals that save the world to-day.
Though men account me nothing, my strength shall be their stay.

But while among my people, made strong in peace, I find
Those things for which I battled, clean life and open mind,
I miss the one fine treasure for which the heathen strove,
The light of happy faces made luminous with love.

"For I who fought so fiercely in my relentless youth
For righteousness of conduct, have come to know this truth:
Ye cannot free man's spirit and leave his senses bound,
Nor leave unused in heaven the joyance of the ground.

Ye shall forego not, therefore, the magic of the spring,
Nor miss one pang of rapture the pagan year can bring;
But build the fairer wisdom that shall emerge at length
Into immortal manhood, whose joy shall be its strength.

"Strive on; still waits perfection; the good fight is not done,
Though we have stretched our borders into the setting sun.
Mistake not great possessions nor might of hand and brain
For hostages of gladness; seek first the surer gain,—

The lightsome heart and sweetness that to the spring belong,
The shine on dappled waters that move both deep and strong."
I glanced round as he pointed to where the river shone,
And when I turned to question him further, he was gone.

A NEW ENGLAND THANKSGIVING

IT is the mellow season
When gold enchantment lies
On stream and road and woodland,
To gladden soul's surmise.
The little old grey homesteads
Are quiet as can be,
Among their stone-fenced orchards
And meadows by the sea.

Here lived the men who gave us
The purpose that holds fast,
The dream that nerves endeavor,
The glory that shall last.
Here strong as pines in winter
And free as ripening corn,

Our faith in fair ideals —
Our fathers' faiths —was born.

Here shone through simple living,
With pride in word and deed,
And consciences of granite,
The old New England breed.
With souls assayed by hardship,
Illumined, self-possessed,
Strongly they lived, and left us
Their passion for the best.

On trails that cut the sunset,
Above the last divide,
The vision has not vanished,
The whisper has not died.
From Shasta to Katahdin,
Blue Hill to Smoky Ridge,
Still stand the just convictions
That stood at Concord Bridge.

Beneath our gilded revel,
Behind our ardent boast,
Above our young impatience
To value least and most,
Sure as the swinging compass
To serve at touch of need,
Square to the world's four corners,
Abides their fearless creed.

Still fired with wonder-working,
Intolerant of peers,
Impetuous and sanguine
After the hundred years,
In likeness to our fathers,
Beyond the safe-marked scope
Of reason and decorum,
We jest and dare and hope.

Thank we the Blood that bred us,
Clear fibre and clean strain —
The Truth which straightly sighted
Lets no one swerve again.
And may almighty Goodness
Give us the will to be
As sweet as upland pastures,
And strong as wind at sea.

IN GOLD LACQUER

Gold are the great trees overhead,
And gold the leaf-strewn grass,
As though a cloth of gold were spread
To let a seraph pass.
And where the pageant should go by,
Meadow and wood and stream,
The world is all of lacquered gold,
Expectant as a dream.

Against the sunset's burning gold,
Etched in dark monotone
Behind its alley of grey trees
And gateposts of grey stone,
Stands the Old Manse, about whose eaves
An air of mystery clings,
Abandoned to the lonely peace
Of bygone ghostly things.

In molten gold the river winds
With languid sweep and turn,
Beside the red-gold wooded hill
Yellowed with ash and fern.
The streets are tiled with gold-green shade
And arched with fretted gold,
Ecstatic aisles that richly thread
This minster grim and old.

The air is flecked with filtered gold, —
The shimmer of romance
Whose ageless glamour still must hold
The world as in a trance,
Pouring o'er every time and place
Light of an amber sea,
The spell of all the gladsome things
That have been or shall be.

MEMORIAL DAY

Once more over relics of winter the willows all gold
Wave odorous plumes of enchantment, the fern-heads unfold
In forgotten places, as fresh as when Pan long ago
Might pass through the bird-haunted woodlands, or linger to blow

On his pure keen pipe by the river. The wild cherry bough
Is robed for the white celebration of memory now.
Old orchards a maze of pink-white with black stems showing through,
Swamp alder and hill-loving birch all betasseled anew,
And ruddy wing-flowering maples, — the year is abloom,
Each dooryard a heaven of lilac, each breeze a perfume.
And hark to the small yellow warbler uplifting his voice,
Serene, so intense, so unstifled! Who could not rejoice
With the splendid oncoming of glory? Tall beech trees are crowned;
Blue violets spring under foot in the magical ground;
And at twilight the frogs will fife up one by one till they fill
The whole dome of dusk with their choral triumphant, to thrill

And transmute to an impulse of gladness the sob in each throat;
As we with proud-spirited music help, too, to denote
And enhance the beneficent wonder, the power of earth
At her sorcery still, bringing ever new triumphs to birth
For the battle-bruised soul, the supreme one, desiring nought
Save that always her truest and goodliest dreams should be wrought
Into loveliness out of this life-stuff. So all things alive,
Birds and winds and the sensitive flowers, persist and survive
With joy unabated, with banners unstruck to the frost,
To remind us no beauty can perish, no effort be lost,
No ardor diminished forever, nor purpose lack room
To accomplish its utmost ideal! As all things resume
Their unfulfilled tasks of perfection, each after its need,
Shall the heart cease from longing, the mind from its loftiest creed,
Or the senses refuse their due service? Behold we arise
From failure, mistake, and regret, putting on the fresh guise
Of a use no disaster can ruin, the ultimate test
When endeavor shall gain all it dreamed of the infinite best, —
The little-regarded and common made great and sublime,
The eternal arrested and fashioned in space and in time.

Then sound a new note on the bugles, unmuffle the drums,
Sing hymns of exulting, proud thanks for the uplift that comes
From the thought of our heroes, resurging like sap in the bough
Through hearts sorrow-hardened and faint, but rehumanized now
By the hand-clasp and rally of loved ones for whom we in trust
Hold sacred ideals bequeathed us from out of the dust
Of battle fields holy. And keep we unfettered and fine
The faith which sustained our strong brothers that truth the divine
Shall unfurl her peace colors, triumphant as blossom and spray,
Bedecking the earth with fresh gladness, and generous as they.

DECORATION DAY

Stand here in the shadow of the Capitol,
And let your eyes range down across the city,
Where marble buildings rise out of a sea
Of tree-tops, and the Monument floats up
All rose and lilac in the morning light,
A thing of magic by the Potomac shore.

Across the river on the wooded bank
Where that colonial portico gleams white,
Is the nation's hallowed ground, —their resting-place
Who gave their lives up gladly for the truth,
Each, as he deemed, a soldier of the right,
Impassioned by the justice of his cause.

And hark, above the car-bells and the cries,
A band is playing! Troops are on the move.
Far down the Avenue a column wheels
To pass the pillared Treasury, on the way
To honor its dead heroes sleeping there
On the heights of Arlington ten thousand strong.

There rests my old friend in his soldier's grave, —
Old grim idealist with the tender heart,
The grizzled head, grey eye, and scanty speech,

And hand that never faltered in the fight
Through all the rough work of a long campaign.
God keep you, General, with the heroes gone!

In many a place through all the land to-day,
Mourners will come, and with hands full of flowers
Pay loving honor to the valiant dead
Who gave their last breath for the cause they loved,
For liberty and justice, and flinched not
To pay the utmost for their noble dream.

And you, O fond and unforgetful ones
Who have no grave to tend for all your loss,
No sacred spot whereat your love may kneel,
But must in silence let the proud tears spring,
Keeping the lonely vigil of the heart,
While the flags flutter and the dead-march plays;

Behold for you the consoling rain shall fall
In odorous assuaging woodland showers,
And wild wood-flowers spring up to deck the ground
Wherever early summer passes now;

And in far valleys where no bugles peal
Shy birds will sing their requiems for your dead.

Therefore, take courage, seeing all natural things
Are not left desolate, but lovely earth
Transmutes each scar and sorrow to her gain,
And from the flux of time and growth renews
Her seasons of indomitable joy,

And breeds new beauty each reviving year.
Let us too live with gladness, and become
A part of that which never can be lost,
But must be merged forever with new power,
The urge, the aspiration, and the gleam, —
All that is infinite and divine in man,
The eternal rescued from mortality.

Let us not doubt, but with an unvexed mind
Bring truth to pass with beauty and with good,
One and sufficient in the last event,
The work made perfect by the loving hand,
The fair ideal translated into fact;
And heaven can not be far from this our world.

And so we turn from memory to-day
To the fresh tasks, splendid heroic toil,
Triumphs of knowledge and beneficence,
And victories unblemished by regret;
With the untroubled confidence of strength
We go to build the commonwealth of peace.

ST. MICHAEL'S STAR

In the pure solitude of dusk
One star is set to shine
Above the sundown's dying rose,
A lamp before a shrine.
It is the star of Michael lit
In the minster of the sun,
That every toiling hand may give
Thanks for the day's work done.

For when the almighty word went forth
To bid creation be, —
The glimmering star-tracks on the blue,
The tide-belts on the sea, —

Perfect as planned, from Michael's hand
The lasting hills arose,
Their bases on the poppied plain,
Their peaks in bannered snows.

Cedar and thorn and oak were born;
Green fiddleheads uncurled
In the spring woods; gold adder-tongues
Came forth to glad the world;—
The magic of the punctual seeds,
Each with its pregnant powers,
As the lord Michael fashioned them
To keep their days and hours.

Frail fins to ride the monstrous tide,
Soft wings to poise and gleam,
He formed the pageant tribe by tribe
As vivid as a dream.
And still must his beneficence
Renew, create, sustain,
The sorcery of the wind and sun,
The alchemy of the rain.

Teeming with God, the kindly sod
Yearns through the summer days
With the mute eloquence of flowers,
Its only means of praise.
At dusk and dawn the tranquil hills
Throb to the song of birds,
And all the dim blue silence thrills
To transport not of words.

For earth must breed to spirit's need,
Clay to the finer clay,
That soul through sense find recompense
And rapture on her way.
And man, from dust and dreaming wrought,
To all things must impart
The trend and likeness of his thought,
The passion of his heart.

The love and lore he shall acquire
To word and deed must dare;
Resemblances of God his sire
His voice and mien must bear.
His children's children shall portray
The skill which he bestows
On living; and what life must mean

His craftsman's instinct knows.

Line upon line and tone by tone,
The visioned form he gives
To sound and color, wood and stone,
Takes loveliness and lives.
He sees his project's soaring hope
Grow substance, and expand
To measure a diviner scope
Beneath his patient hand.

To pencil, brush, and burnisher
His wizardry he lends,
And to the care of lathe and loom
His secret he commends.
In hues and forms and cadences
New beauty he instills,
A brother by the right of craft
To Michael of the hills.

EASTER EVE

If I should tell you I saw Pan lately down by the shallows of Silvermine,
Blowing an air on his pipe of willow, just as the moon began to shine;
Or say that, coming from town on Wednesday, I met Christ walking in Ponus Street;
You might remark, "Our friend is flighty! Visions, for want of enough red meat!"

Then let me ask you. Last December, when there was skating on Wampanaw,
Among the weeds and sticks and grasses under the hard black ice I saw
An old mud-turtle poking about, as if he were putting his house to rights,
Stiff with the cold perhaps, yet knowing enough to prepare for the winter nights.

And here he is on a log this morning, sunning himself as calm as you please.
But I want to know, when the lock of winter was sprung of a sudden, who kept the keys?
Who told old nibbler to go to sleep safe and sound with the lily roots,
And then in the first warm days of April —out to the sun with the greening shoots?

By night a flock of geese went over, honking north on the trails of air,
The spring express —but who despatched it, equipped with speed and cunning care?
Hark to our bluebird down in the orchard trolling his chant of the happy heart,
As full of light as a theme of Mozart's —but where did he learn that more than art?

Where the river winds through grassy meadows, as sure as the south wind brings the rain,
Sounding his reedy note in the alders, the starling comes back to his nest again.
Are these not miracles? Prompt you answer: "Merely the prose of natural fact;
Nothing but instinct plain and patent, born in the creatures, that bids them act."

Well, I have an instinct as fine and valid, surely, as that of the beasts and birds,
Concerning death and the life immortal, too deep for logic, too vague for words.
No trace of beauty can pass or perish, but other beauty is somewhere born;
No seed of truth or good be planted, but the yield must grow as the growing corn.

Therefore this ardent mind and spirit I give to the glowing days of earth,
To be wrought by the Lord of life to something of lasting import and lovely worth.
If the toil I give be without self-seeking, bestowed to the limit of will and power,
To fashion after some form ideal the instant task and the waiting hour,

It matters not though defeat undo me, though faults betray me and sorrows scar,
Already I share the life eternal with the April buds and the evening star.
Our minister here, entrenched in doctrine, may know no doubt upon Easter Eve.
And when it comes to the crucial question, Doctor, you skeptic, you too believe!

RESURGAM

Lo, now comes the April pageant
And the Easter of the year.
Now the tulip lifts her chalice,
And the hyacinth his spear;
All the daffodils and jonquils
With their hearts of gold are here.
Child of the immortal vision,
What hast thou to do with fear?

When the summons wakes the impulse,
And the blood beats in the vein,
Let no grief thy dream encumber,
No regret thy thought detain.
Through the scented bloom-hung valleys,
Over tillage, wood and plain,
Comes the soothing south wind laden
With the sweet impartial rain.

All along the roofs and pavements
Pass the volleying silver showers,
To unfold the hearts of humans
And the frail unanxious flowers.
Breeding fast in sunlit places,
Teeming life puts forth her powers,
And the migrant wings come northward
On the trail of golden hours.

Over intervale and upland

Sounds the robin's interlude
From his tree-top spire at evening
Where no unbeliefs intrude.
Every follower of beauty
Finds in the spring solitude
Sanctuary and persuasion
Where the mysteries still brood.

Now the bluebird in the orchard,
A warm sighing at the door,
And the soft haze on the hillside,
Lure the houseling to explore
The perennial enchanted
Lovely world and all its lore;
While the early tender twilight
Breathes of those who come no more.

By full brimming river margins
Where the scents of brush fires blow,
Through the faint green mist of springtime,
Dreaming glad-eyed lovers go,
Touched with such immortal madness
Not a thing they care to know
More than those who caught life's secret
Countless centuries ago.

In old Egypt for Osiris,
Putting on the green attire,
With soft hymns and choric dancing
They went forth to greet the fire
Of the vernal sun, whose ardor
His earth children could inspire;
And the ivory flutes would lead them
To the slake of their desire.

In remembrance of Adonis
Did the Dorian maidens sing
Linus songs of joy and sorrow
For the coming back of spring, —
Sorrow for the wintry death
Of each irrevocable thing,
Joy for all the pangs of beauty
The returning year could bring.

Now the priests and holy women
With sweet incense, chant and prayer,
Keep His death and resurrection
Whose new love bade all men share

Immortality of kindness,
Living to make life more fair.
Wakened to such wealth of being,
Who would not arise and dare?

Seeing how each new fulfillment
Issues at the call of need
From infinitudes of purpose
In the core of soul and seed,
Who shall set the bounds of puissance
Or the formulas of creed?
Truth awaits the test of beauty,
Good is proven in the deed.

Therefore, give thy spring renascence, —
Freshened ardor, dreams and mirth, —
To make perfect and replenish
All the sorry fault and dearth
Of the life from whose enrichment
Thine aspiring will had birth;
Take thy part in the redemption
Of thy kind from bonds of earth.

So shalt thou, absorbed in beauty,
Even in this mortal clime
Share the life that is eternal,
Brother to the lords of time, —
Virgil, Raphael, Gautama, —
Builders of the world sublime.
Yesterday was not earth's evening,
Every morning is our prime.

All that can be worth the rescue
From oblivion and decay, —
Joy and loveliness and wisdom, —
In thyself, without dismay
Thou shalt save and make enduring
Through each word and act, to sway
The hereafter to a likeness
Of thyself in other clay.

Still remains the peradventure,
Soul pursues an orbit here
Like those unreturning comets,
Sweeping on a vast career,
By an infinite directrix,
Focussed to a finite sphere, —
Nurtured in an earthly April,

In what realm to reappear?

AT THE MAKING OF MAN

First all the host of Raphael
In liveries of gold,
Lifted the chorus on whose rhythm
The spinning spheres are rolled, —
The Seraphs of the morning calm
Whose hearts are never cold.

He shall be born a spirit,
Part of the soul that yearns,
The core of vital gladness
That suffers and discerns,
The stir that breaks the budding sheath
When the green spring returns, —

The gist of power and patience
Hid in the plasmic clay,
The calm behind the senses,
The passionate essay
To make his wise and lovely dream
Immortal on a day.

The soft Aprilian ardors
That warm the waiting loam
Shall whisper in his pulses
To bid him overcome,
And he shall learn the wonder-cry
Beneath the azure dome.

And though all-dying nature
Should teach him to deplore,
The ruddy fires of autumn
Shall lure him but the more
To pass from joy to stronger joy,
As through an open door.

He shall have hope and honor,
Proud trust and courage stark,
To hold him to his purpose
Through the unlighted dark,
And love that sees the moon's full orb
In the first silver arc.

And he shall live by kindness
And the heart's certitude,
Which moves without misgiving
In ways not understood,
Sure only of the vast event,—
The large and simple good.

Then Gabriel's host in silver gear
And vesture twilight blue,
The spirits of immortal mind,
The warders of the true,
Took up the theme that gives the world
Significance anew.

He shall be born to reason,
And have the primal need
To understand and follow
Wherever truth may lead,—
To grow in wisdom like a tree
Unfolding from a seed.

A watcher by the sheepfolds,
With wonder in his eyes,
He shall behold the seasons,
And mark the planets rise,
Till all the marching firmament
Shall rouse his vast surmise.

Beyond the sweep of vision,
Or utmost reach of sound,
This cunning fire-maker,
This tiller of the ground,
Shall learn the secrets of the suns
And fathom the profound.

For he must prove all being
Sane, beauteous, benign,
And at the heart of nature
Discover the divine, —
Himself the type and symbol
Of the eternal trine.

He shall perceive the kindling
Of knowledge, far and dim,
As of the fire that brightens
Below the dark sea-rim,
When ray by ray the splendid sun
Floats to the world's wide brim.

And out of primal instinct,
The lore of lair and den,
He shall emerge to question
How, wherefore, whence, and when,
Till the last frontier of the truth
Shall lie within his ken.

Then Michael's scarlet-suited host
Took up the word and sang;
As though a trumpet had been loosed
In heaven, the arches rang;
For these were they who feel the thrill
Of beauty like a pang.

He shall be framed and balanced
For loveliness and power,
Lithe as the supple creatures,
And colored as a flower,
Sustained by the all-feeding earth,
Nurtured by wind and shower,

To stand within the vortex
Where surging forces play,
A poised and pliant figure
Immutable as they,
Till time and space and energy
Surrender to his sway.

He shall be free to journey
Over the teeming earth,
An insatiable seeker,
A wanderer from his birth,
Clothed in the fragile veil of sense,
With fortitude for girth.

His hands shall have dominion
Of all created things,
To fashion in the likeness
Of his imaginings,
To make his will and thought survive
Unto a thousand springs.

The world shall be his province,
The princedom of his skill;
The tides shall wear his harness,
The winds obey his will;
Till neither flood, nor fire, nor frost,

Shall work to do him ill.

A creature fit to carry
The pure creative fire,
Whatever truth inform him,
Whatever good inspire,
He shall make lovely in all things
To the end of his desire.

ON PONUS RIDGE

I heard the voice of our mother planet murmur today as the south wind blew
Over the old Connecticut granite, up from the Sound and the rainy blue.
"What is your comment, wandering brother," said Ponus Ridge to the striding rain,
"Not on the new word, Love one another, but the harder text, Ye shall rise again?

"Hast thou found out truth at the core of being, in thy long wandering to and fro?
Dost thou know what lurks beyond foreseeing in the endless rhythm of ebb and flow?"
"Much have I heard," said Rain, "of the babel and heated haste of the lordling Man,
Telling the wind his gorgeous fable; but who shall hurry or check the plan?

"'I take small heed of the tales he mutters," the glittering copious rain ran on;
"My music drowns the words he utters; I make my bed where his town-lights shone.
I hear the drone of his church and college, humming like hives from roof to floor
With direful chant and delirious knowledge, as I pass foot-free by their open door.

"I have heard the vaunts of his daring dreamers, the things foretold by his sons of might,
And watched him flaunt like the boreal streamers that glow and fade in the arctic night.
I have seen the flare of his pageants kindled, the pride of Carthage, the pomp of Tyre;
And even as I fell they sank and dwindled, beaten down like a farm-boy's fire.

"The earth is my house, the spring my portal; I serve without envy, debate or fear.
Though I pass in mist, am I less immortal than the greatening germ or the glowing sphere?
I come from the sea and I go to the sea; ten thousand times have I risen again
From the welter and lift of eternity, to solace thy waiting not in vain.

"My strength is loosed for thy brooks and rivers, by lake and orchard, by wood and field;
My silver voice with a sob delivers the message for telling a goodly yield.
I have quickened the joy in thy swelling breast, I have sluiced the ache of thy breeding fire;
I have perished in transport and died with zest, to fill the measure of thy desire.

"The seeds of life are of my sowing, the virile impulse, the fertile gush,
The gist and start of all things growing; but thine is the warmth and the pregnant hush.
The stir of joy is of my giving; a hint of perfection far and fine
I speak as I pass to all things living; but the patient wisdom and lore are thine."

Then the mother granite, grey, eternal, scarred, to the careless eye uncouth,
Spoke in a language pure and vernal, solemn as beauty and sweet as truth.
In the voice of the Ridge in her April season, through the babble of streams and the calls of birds,
Under the rune I caught the reason, out of the murmur I made the words.

"Nay, my comrade, I too must pass; though my fleeting hours be ages long,
I abide in the end no more than the grass, than a puff of smoke or a strain of song.
If I give myself to the moment's rapture of lilt and leafage, shall I repine
That the joy I bestow escapes recapture, spent for the beauty of branch and vine?

"Strong, unhurrying, unbelated, part of the slow sidereal urge,
Patient and sure at heart I waited for life to throb and its forms emerge.
While cosmic aeons dawned and darkened, and monstrous drift and blast went by,
In my slow gestation I lay and harkened for soul to question and sense to cry.
"I am the ardent and ageless mother of all things human, all things divine.
The ravaging snows may whirl and smother, the large cold moon of November shine,
But safe in my soil the germs are sleeping that shall awake when the time is come,
To prove the beneficence of my keeping, and don the glory of fragrant bloom.

"See my young willows in sunlight lifting their silver lances against the blue,
And here where the matted leaves are rifting, the hoods of the blood-root breaking through.
Soon in the sheltered sun-warmed places, out of my ancient enchanted mould,
Frail spring-beauties will lift their faces, and adder-tongues put forth their gold.

"Hark to my minstrel, beyond the boulders down in the swamp, — on time, no fear!—
In his sable coat with scarlet shoulders, with his husky flute that is good to hear.
And hark again, in the long Aprilian dusk on the marsh to my piper's cry.
To-night but one, to-morrow a million will lift my heart on their chorus high.

"Now Sirius low in the west is leaning, Arcturus lifts on the eastern rim, —
The poise, the order, the mighty meaning, creating beauty from brim to brim.
Under the dust of seed and planet, the river music, the starry light,
Am I in the midst, immortal granite, merging my strength with the soul of night.

"At morn I shall see from my stream-bed narrow the wild geese flapping with honk and plash,
To steady and drive their Indian arrow north-by-east for the Allegash.
And then the high clear note of gladness, the rallying call of the golden-wing,
The solace of grief, the shame of sadness, the goodly far-sent summons of spring.

"Here all day long I shall lie and ponder the teeming life whereon I brood,
While the buds unfold, the low clouds wander, and all things flow to rhythm and mood.
And seeing all form but the trace of motion, all beauty the vestige of joy made plain,
Shall I stint my care and my devotion, to vex me with counting the once or again?

"I take no measure, I keep no tally, of the budding spray and the leafing bough,
Yet not a blossom in all the valley but is the pride of' my patience now.
In the hardwood groves where the sun lies mellow, the purple hepaticas take the air.
I help the catkins to break and yellow; the greening spring-runs are in my care.

"I loosen the sheaths of the bladed rushes, I lift the sap in the spiral cells,
Till the first soft tinge through the woodland flushes, and the crimson bud of the maple swells.
I nurse them to beauty hour by hour. And there by the road in its grove of pine,
The little bare school with its dreams of power and joy of knowledge, — that, too, is mine!"

THE MAN OF PEACE

What winter holiday is this?
In Time's great calendar,
Marked in the rubric of the saints,
And with a soldier's star,
Here stands the name of one who lived
To serve the common weal,
With humor tender as a prayer
And honor firm as steel.

No hundred hundred years can dim
The radiance of his mirth,
That set unselfish laughter free
From all the sons of earth.
Unswerved through stress and scant success,
Out of his dreamful youth
He kept an unperverted faith
In the almighty truth.

Born in the fulness of the days,
Up from the teeming soil,
By the world-mother reared and schooled
In reverence and toil,
He stands the test of all life's best
Through play, defeat, or strain;
Never a moment was he found
Unlovable nor vain.

Fondly we set apart this day,
And mark this plot of earth
To be forever hallowed ground
In honor of his birth,
Where men may come as to a shrine
And temple of the good,
To be made sweet and strong of heart
In Lincoln's brotherhood.

Here walked God's earth in modesty
The shadow that was man,

A shade of the divine that moved
Through His mysterious plan.
So must we fill the larger mould
Of wisdom, love, and power,
Fearless, compassionate, contained,
And masters of the hour,

As men found faithful to a task
Eternal, pressing, plain,
Accounting manhood more than wealth,
And gladness more than gain;
Distilling happiness from life,
As vigor from the air,
Not wresting it with ruthless hands,
Spoiling our brother's share.

Here shall our children keep alive
The passion for the right,—
The cause of justice in the world,
That was our fathers' fight.
For this the fair-haired stripling rode,
The dauntless veteran died,
For this we keep the ancient code
In stubbornness and pride.

O South, bring all your chivalry;
And West, give all your heart;
And East, your old untarnished dreams
Of progress and of art!
Bid waste and war to be no more,
Bid wanton riot cease;
At your command give Lincoln's land
To Paradise, — to peace.

CHAMPLAIN

When the sweet Summer days
Come to New England, and the south wind plays
Over the forests, and the tall tulip trees
Lift up their chalices
Of delicate orange green
Against the blue serene;
When the chestnut crowns are full of flowers,
And the long hours
Are not too long
For the oriole's song;

When the wild roses blow
In blueberry pastures, and the Bobwhite's note
Calls us away
On the happy trail where every heart must go;
When the white clouds float
Through an ampler day,
Above the battlements of the Mountains Green,
Where the woods come down to the fields on every hand,
And the meadow-land
Breaks into ripples and swells
With the gold of the black-eyed daisies and lily-bells;
When the old.sea lies mystical blue once more
Along the Pilgrim shore,
Crooning to stone-fenced pastures sweet with fern
Tales of the long ago and the far away;

And when to the hemlock solitudes return
The gold-voiced thrushes, and the high beach woods
Ring with enchantment as the twilight falls
Among the darkening hills;
And the new moonlight fills
The world with beauty and the soul with peace
And infinite release;
Is there any land that history recalls,
Bestowed by gods on mortals anywhere,
More goodly than New England or more fair?

On such a day three hundred years ago
By toilsome trails and slow,
But with the adventurer's spirit high aflame,
The great discoverer came,
Finding another Indies than he guessed
To reward his daring quest,
And fill the wonder-volume of Romance, —
The sailor of little Brouage, the founder of New France,
Sturdy, sagacious, plain
Samuel de Champlain.

On many a river and stream
The paddles of his Abenakis dip and gleam;
Their slim canoe-poles set and flash in the sun,
Where strong white waters run;

By many a portage, many a wooded shore,
They press on to explore
The unknown that leads them ever to the west;
And when at dusk their camp is made
Within the dense still shade,

The white shafts of the moonlight creep
About them while they sleep
On the earth's fragrant and untroubled breast.
Then on a day upon some marble rise
They stand in mute surmise,
And wonder, as they gaze
On the green wilderness in summer haze,
At a new paradise
Unrolled before their eyes.

What did he seek,
This hardy voyager with the steady hand,
And the sunburnt cheek?

Passage to India and the fabled land
So longed for and foretold,
Where rivers ran with gold, —
Man's fond far hope of unlaborious ease,
Miraculous wealth and benefits unearned,
For which he vainly yearned.

He found here no such place,
But in this new world again was face to face
With life's familiar laws and orders old,
Still to be followed, if we would fill the mould
Of our ideal, —a manhood that is free
With the soul's large and happy liberty.

As if God said to Man,
"Try once again my plan.
Here is a continent all new,
Take it and see once more what thou canst do.
The happiness which thy stormy heart desires
My will foresees, requires.
On the long road that lies
Across the centuries
To my perfection dimly understood,
Seek thou the almighty good,
The everlasting beautiful and true."

Men of New England, sons of pioneers,
And in your birthright peers
Of the world's masters, this is holy soil,
The divine ancestral dust from which we come,
Bringing our dream of justice, the high thought
Of a pure freedom for which our mothers wrought
In dreamful pride,
And our fathers lived and died

With unselfish toil.

Even as they willed,
We too must toil to build
The ideal state,
Which shall be strong without brutality,
And by its fine humanity be great.

This is no fairyland,
No Eldorado planned
For man's salvation. The law runs forth and back,
Immutable as the sun on his sidereal track,
Beneficent as the trees,
And as the noon profound:
Only with labor comes ease,
Only with wisdom comes joy,
And greatness comes not without love.

This is God's garden ground,
And we are the tillers thereof.
And the crop shall be women and men,
As ever of old, —
Not a pale city breed,
Bred between hunger and greed,
But a new cosmic race,
With the poise of the world in its mien,
The ineffable soul in its face,
Remembering the best that has been,
And its password, "The best that can be!"

No Mesopotamian valley, nor Eden age,
No long ago, nor by-and-by,
Is the place, is the time,
For the birth of the sublime
From the lovely and the sane.
But the time is now, and the place is here,
For life divine,
In July of the year
Nineteen hundred and nine,
In the Country of Champlain.

THE GOLDEN WEST

I.

In the golden dawn of the world,

When man emerged
From the mysterious East,
With the breath of life in his mouth,
And the tell-tale trace
Of the red clay still on his face.

He turned with inquisitive gaze,
A child of the light,
To follow the track of the sun
Through the void far blue,
Seeing it sink to rest
In a glorious golden West.

Then an unassuageable urge
Awoke in his blood,
The brooding spirit of Earth
Whispered a word in his heart,
And man went forth on the trail,
Knowing he should not fail.

II.

And the slow centuries
Measured his toilsome march,
While ever his face was set

To lands that lie beyond
The going down of the sun,
Where endeavor's requital is won.

From Egypt and Greece and Tyre,
From Assyria and Rome,
With color and pomp and joy,
Laughter and chants and war,
Moved the great caravan
Of wandering man.

Conquering mountain and sea,
Spreading through forest and plain,
Crossing the outer flood,—
The rim of the ancient world,—
He passed over new domain
Like the hosts of sweeping rain.

Traversing prairie and wood,
Waterway, desert, and range,
At last by the ultimate shore

Of the ageless sea,
His pack-trains come to rest
In our golden West.

III.

Here have the most high Ones,
The Overlords of the world,
The Archangels of man,
Brought their earth children at last,
To the happy land prepared
For those who have labored and dared.

O men and women born
Of the teeming and holy earth,
And led through the myriad years
By the impulse and vision divine,
Behold now what shall be done
With the heritage we have won?

Here with an empire to use,
Wealth beyond Solomon's dream,
And the balm and respite of peace,
In a garden of the world,
What is the news or the plan
Of Twentieth Century man?

IV.

I heard the Sierras reply,
Rank after rank as they rose
Through the golden and violet light,

"The destined days are at hand,
When my children shall arise
And assume the heroic guise

"From the beginning designed
For the seraphs, and sons of earth.
They shall put off envy and fear,
And skulking merciless greed,
And be girded against all ills
With the vigor and poise of the hills.

"Here on this border of time
Where mighty morrows are born,

Emerging from ages of dream
And the dust of unreason and strife,
They shall grow wise and humane
With a gladness virile and sane.

"Primal in beauty and pride,
Christian in kindness and calm,
Modern in knowledge and skill,
Sons of the morning, arise —
Earth's awaited and best —
From the golden West!"

THE GATE OF PEACE

Ah, who will build the city of our dream,
Where beauty shall abound and truth avail,
With patient love that is too wise for strife,
Blending in power as gentle as the rain
With the reviving earth on full spring days?
Who now will speed us to its gate of peace,
And reassure us on our doubtful road?

Three centuries ago a fearless man,
Yearning to set his people in the way,
Threw all his royal might into a plan
To found an ideal city that should give
Freedom to every instinct for the best,
From humblest impulse in his own domain
To rumored wisdom from the world's far ends.
Strengthened with ardor from a high resolve,
Beneath the patient smile of Indian skies
This fair dream flourished for a score of years,
Until the blight of evil touched its bloom
With fading, and transformed its vivid life
Into a ghost-flower of its fair design.

Now ruined nursery tower and gay boudoir,
A sad custodian of sacred tombs,
And scattered feathers from the purple wings
Of doves who reign in undisputed calm
Over this Eden of hope and fair essay,
Recall the valor of this ancient quest.

Great Akbar, —grandfather of Shah Jehan,
The artist Emperor of India
Who built the Taj for love of one held dear

Beyond all other women in the world,
And left that loveliest memorial,
The most supreme of wonders wrought by man,
To move for very joy all hearts to tears
Beholding how great beauty springs from love, —
Akbar the wisest ruler over Ind,
Grandson of Babar in whose veins were mixed
The blood of Tamerlane and Chinghiz Khan,
Who beat the Afghans and the Rajputs down
At Paniput and Buxar in Bengal,
Making himself the lord of Hindustan,
And with his restless Tartars founded there
The Mogul empire with its Moslem faith,
Its joyousness, enlightenment, and art, —
Akbar of all the sovereigns of the East
Is still most deeply loved and gladly praised.

For he who conquered with so strong a hand
Cabul, Kashmir, and Kandahar, and Sind,
Oudh and Orissa, Chitor and Ajmir,
With all their wealth to weld them into one,
Upholding justice with his sovereignty
Throughout his borders and imposing peace,
Was first and last a seeker after truth.

No craven unlaborious truce he sought,
But that great peace which only comes with light,
Emerging after chaos has been quelled
In some long struggle of enduring will,
To be a proof of order and of law,
Which cannot rest on falsehood nor on wrong,
But spreads like generous sunshine on the earth
When goodness has been gained and truth made clear,
At whatsoe'er incalculable cost.

Returning once with his victorious arms
And war-worn companies on the homeward march
To Agra and his court's magnificence,
From a campaign against some turbulent folk,
He came at evening to a quiet place
Near Sikri by the roadside through the woods,
Where there were many doves among the trees.

There Salim Chisti a holy man had made
His lonely dwelling in the wilderness,
Seeking perfection. And the solitude
Was sweet to Akbar, and he halted there
And went to Salim in his lodge and said,

"O man and brother, thy long days are spent
In meditation, seeking for the path

Through this great world's impediments to peace,
Here in the twilight with the holy stars
Or when the rose of morning breaks in gold;
Tell me, I pray, whence comes the gift of peace
With all its blessings for a people's need,
And how may true tranquillity be found
On which man's restless spirit longs to rest?"

And Salim answered, "Lord, most readily
In Allah's out-of-doors, for there men live
More truly, being free from false constraint,
For learning wisdom with a calmer mind.
For they who would find peace must conquer fear
And ignorance and greed, — the ravagers
Of spirit, mind, and sense, — and learn to live
Content beneath the shade of Allah's' hand.
Who worships not his own will shall find peace."

Then Akbar answered, "I have set my heart
On making beauty, truth, and justice shine
As the ordered stars above the darkened earth.
Are not these also things to be desired,
And striven for with no uncertain toil?
And save through them whence comes the gift of peace?"

Then Salim smiled, and with his finger drew
In the soft dust before his door, and said,
"O king, thy words are true, thy heart most wise.
Thou also shalt find peace, as Allah wills,
Through following bravely what to thee seems best.
When any question, 'What is peace?' reply,
'The shelter of the Gate of Paradise,
The shadow of the archway, not the arch,
Within whose shade at need the poor may rest,
The weary be refreshed, the weak secure,
And all men pause to gladden as they go.'"

And Akbar pondered Salim Chisti's words.
Then turning to his ministers, he said,
"Here will I build my capital, and here
The world shall come unto a council hall,
And in a place of peace pursue the quest
Of wisdom and the finding out of truth,
That there be no more discord upon earth,
But only knowledge, beauty, and good will."

And it was done according to Akbar's word.
There in the wilderness as by magic rose
Futtehpur Sikri, the victorious city,
Of marble and red sandstone among the trees,

A rose unfolding in the kindling dawn.
Palace and mosque and garden and serai,
Bazaars and baths and spacious pleasure grounds,
By favor of Allah to perfection sprang.

Thus Akbar wrought to make his dream come true.
From the four corners of the world he brought
His master workmen, from Iran and Ind,
From wild Mongolia and the Arabian wastes;
Masons from Baghdad, Delhi, and Multan;
Dome builders from the North, from Samarkand;
Cunning mosaic workers from Kanauj;
And carvers of inscriptions from Shiraz;.
An'd they all labored with enduring skill,
Each at his handicraft, to make beauty be.

When the first ax-blade on the timber rang,
The timid doves, as if foreboding ill,
Had fled from Sikri and its quiet groves.

But as he promised, Akbar sent and bade
The wise men of all nations to his court,
Brahman and Christian, Buddhist and Parsee,
Jain and stiff Mohammedan and Jew,
All followers of the One with many names,
Bringing the ghostly wisdom of the earth.

And so they came of every hue and creed.
From the twelve winds of heaven their caravans
Drew into Sikri as Akbar summoned them,
To spend long afternoons in council grave,
Sifting tradition for the seed of truth,
In the great mosque in Futtehpur at peace.
And Salim Chisti lived his holy life,
Beloved and honored there as Akbar's friend.

But light and changeable are the hearts of men.
Soon in that city dedicate to peace
Dissensions spread and rivalries grew rife,
Envy and bitterness and strife returned
Once more, and truth before them fled away.

Then Salim Chisti, coming to Akbar spoke,
"Lord, give thy servant leave now to depart
And follow where the fluttered wings have gone,
For here there is no longer any peace,
And truth cannot prevail where discord dwells."

"Nay then," said Akbar, "'tis not thou but I
Who am the servant here and must go hence.
I found thee master of this solitude,
Lord of the princedom of a quiet mind,
A sovereign vested in tranquillity,
And I have done thee wrong and stayed thy feet
From following perfection, with my horde

Of turbulent malcontents; and my loved dream
To build a city of abiding peace
Was but a vain illusion. Therefore now
This foolish people shall be driven forth
From this fair place, to live as they may choose
In disputance and wrangling longer still,
Until they learn, if Allah wills it so,
To lay aside their folly for the truth."

And as the king commanded, so it was.
More quickly than he came, with all his court
And hosts of followers he went away,
Leaving the place to solitude once more,—
A rose to wither where it once had blown.

To-day the all-kind unpolluted sun
Shines through the marble fret-work with no sound;
The winds play hide and seek through corridors
Where stately women with dark glowing eyes
Have laughed and frolicked in their fluttering robes;
The rose leaves drop with none to gather them,
In gardens where no footfall comes with eve,
Nor any lovers watch the rising moon;
And ancient silence, truer than all speech,
Still holds the secrets of the Council Hall,
Upon whose walls frescoes of many faiths
Attest the courtesy of open minds.

Before the last camp-follower was gone,
The doves returned and took up their abode
In the main gate of those deserted walls.
And in their custody this "Gate of Peace"
Bears still the grandeur of its origin,
Firing anew the wistful hearts of men

To brave endeavor with replenished hope,
Though since that time three hundred years ago,
The magic hush of those forsaken streets
And empty courtyards has been undisturbed
Save by the gentle whirring of grey wings,
With cooing murmurs uttered all day long,
And reverent tread of those from near and far,
Who still pursue the immemorial quest.

THE TWELFTH NIGHT STAR

It is the bitter time of year
When iron is the ground,
With hasp and sheathing of black ice
The forest lakes are bound,
The world lies snugly under snow,
Asleep without a sound.

All the night long in trooping squares
The sentry stars go by,
The silent and unwearying hosts
That bear man company,
And with their pure enkindling fires
Keep vigils lone and high.

Through the dead hours before the dawn,
When the frost snaps the sill,
From chestnut-wooded ridge to sea
The earth lies dark and still,
Till one great silver planet shines
Above the eastern hill.

It is the star of Gabriel,
The herald of the Word
In days when messengers of God
With sons of men conferred,
Who brought the tidings of great joy
The watching shepherds heard;

The mystic light that moved to lead
The wise of long ago,
Out of the great East where they dreamed
Of truths they could not know,
To seek some good that should assuage
The world's most ancient woe.

O well, believe, they loved their dream,
Those children of the star,
Who saw the light and followed it,
Prophetical, afar,—
Brave Gaspar, clear-eyed Melchior,
And eager Balthasar.

Another year slips to the void,
And still with omen bright
Above the sleeping doubting world
The day-star is alight,—
The waking signal flashed of old
In the blue Syrian night.

But who are now as wise as they
Whose faith could read the sign
Of the three gifts that shall suffice
To honor the divine,
And show the trend of common life
Ineffably benign?

Whoever wakens on a day
Happy to know and be,
To enjoy the air, to love his kind,
To labor, to be free,—
Already his enraptured soul
Lives in eternity.

For him with every rising sun
The year begins anew;
The fertile earth receives her lord,
And prophecy comes true,
Wondrously as a fall of snow,
Dear as a drench of dew.
Who gives his life for beauty's need,
King Gaspar could no more;

Who serves the truth with single mind
Shall stand with Melchior;
And love is all that Balthasar
In crested censer bore.

Bliss Carman - An Appreciation

How many Canadians—how many even among the few who seek to keep themselves informed of the
best in contemporary literature, who are ever on the alert for the new voices—realise, or even suspect,

that this Northern land of theirs has produced a poet of whom it may be affirmed with confidence and assurance that he is of the great succession of English poets? Yet such—strange and unbelievable though it may seem—is in very truth the case, that poet being (to give him his full name) William Bliss Carman. Canada has full right to be proud of her poets, a small body though they are; but not only does Mr. Carman stand high and clear above them all—his place (and time cannot but confirm and justify the assertion) is among those men whose poetry is the shining glory of that great English literature which is our common heritage.

If any should ask why, if what has been just said is so, there has been—as must be admitted—no general recognition of the fact in the poet's home land, I would answer that there are various and plausible, if not good, reasons for it.

First of all, the poet, as thousands more of our young men of ambition and confidence have done, went early to the United States, and until recently, except for rare and brief visits to his old home down by the sea, has never returned to Canada—though for all that, I am able to state, on his own authority, he is still a Canadian citizen. Then all his books have had their original publication in the United States, and while a few of them have subsequently carried the imprints of Canadian publishers, none of these can be said ever to have made any special effort to push their sale. Another reason for the fact above mentioned is that Mr. Carman has always scorned to advertise himself, while his work has never been the subject of the log-rolling and booming which the work of many another poet has had—to his ultimate loss. A further reason is that he follows a rule of his own in preparing his books for publication. Most poets publish a volume of their work as soon as, through their industry and perseverance, they have material enough on hand to make publication desirable in their eyes. Not so with Mr. Carman, however, his rule being not to publish until he has done sufficient work of a certain general character or key to make a volume. As a result, you cannot fully know or estimate his work by one book, or two books, or even half a dozen; you must possess or be familiar with every one of the score and more volumes which contain his output of poetry before you can realise how great and how many-sided is his genius.

It is a common remark on the part of those who respond readily to the vigorous work of Kipling, or Masefield, even our own Service, that Bliss Carman's poetry has no relation to or concern with ordinary, everyday life. One would suppose that most persons who cared for poetry at all turned to it as a relief from or counter to the burdens and vexations of the daily round; but in any event, the remark referred to seems to me to indicate either the most casual acquaintance with Mr. Carman's work, or a complete misunderstanding and misapprehension of the meaning of it. I grant that you will find little or nothing in it all to remind you of the grim realities and vexing social problems of this modern existence of ours; but to say or to suggest that these things do not exist for Mr. Carman is to say or to suggest something which is the reverse of true. The truth is, he is aware of them as only one with the sensitive organism of a poet can be; but he does not feel that he has a call or mission to remedy them, and still less to sing of them. He therefore leaves the immediate problems of the day to those who choose, or are led, to occupy themselves therewith, and turns resolutely away to dwell upon those things which for him possess infinitely greater importance.

"What are they?" one who knows Mr. Carman only as, say, a lyrist of spring or as a singer of the delights of vagabondia probably will ask in some wonder. Well, the things which concern him above all, I would answer, are first, and naturally, the beauty and wonder of this world of ours, and next the mystery of the earthly pilgrimage of the human soul out of eternity and back into it again.

The poems in the present volume—which, by the way, can boast the high honor of being the very first regular Canadian edition of his work—will be evidence ample and conclusive to every reader, I am sure, of the place which

The perennial enchanted
Lovely world and all its lore

occupy in the heart and soul of Bliss Carman, as well as of the magical power with which he is able to convey the deep and unfailing satisfaction and delight which they possess for him. They, however, represent his latest period (he has had three well-defined periods), comprising selections from three of his last published volumes: The Rough Rider, Echoes from Vagabondia, and April Airs, together with a number of new poems, and do not show, except here and there and by hints and flashes, how great is his preoccupation with the problem of man's existence—

—the hidden import
Of man's eternal plight.

This is manifest most in certain of his earlier books, for in these he turns and returns to the greatest of all the problems of man almost constantly, probing, with consummate and almost unrivalled use of the art of expression, for the secret which surely, he clearly feels, lies hidden somewhere, to be discovered if one could but pierce deeply enough. Pick up Behind the Arras, and as you turn over page after page you cannot but observe how incessantly the poet's mind—like the minds of his two great masters, Browning and Whitman—works at this problem. In "Behind the Arras," the title poem; "In the Wings," "The Crimson House," "The Lodger," "Beyond the Gamut," "The Juggler"—yes, in every poem in the book—he takes up and handles the strange thing we know as, or call, life, turning it now this way, now that, in an effort to find out its meaning and purpose. He comes but little nearer success in this than do most of the rest of men, of course; but the magical and ever-fresh beauty of his expression, the haunting melody of his lines, the variety of his images and figures and the depth and range of his thought, put his searchings and ponderings in a class by themselves.

Lengthy quotation from Mr. Carman's books is not permitted here, and I must guide myself accordingly, though with reluctance, because I believe that in a study such as this the subject should be allowed to speak for himself as much as possible. In "Behind the Arras" the poet describes the passage from life to death as

A cadence dying down unto its source
In music's course,

and goes on to speak of death as

—the broken rhythm of thought and man,
The sweep and span
Of memory and hope
About the orbit where they still must grope
For wider scope,

To be through thousand springs restored, renewed,
With love imbrued,

With increments of will
Made strong, perceiving unattainment still
From each new skill.

Now follow some verses from "Behind the Gamut," to my mind the poet's greatest single achievement;

As fine sand spread on a disc of silver,
At some chord which bids the motes combine,
Heeding the hidden and reverberant impulse,
Shifts and dances into curve and line,

The round earth, too, haply, like a dust-mote,
Was set whirling her assigned sure way,
Round this little orb of her ecliptic
To some harmony she must obey.

And what of man?

Linked to all his half-accomplished fellows,
Through unfrontiered provinces to range—
Man is but the morning dream of nature,
Roused to some wild cadence weird and strange.

Here, now, are some verses from "Pulvis et Umbra," which is to be found in Mr. Carman's first book, Low Tide on Grand Pré, and in which the poet addresses a moth which a storm has blown into his window:

For man walks the world with mourning
Down to death and leaves no trace,
With the dust upon his forehead,
And the shadow on his face.

Pillared dust and fleeing shadow
As the roadside wind goes by,
And the fourscore years that vanish
In the twinkling of an eye.

"Pillared dust and fleeing shadow." Where in all our English literature will one find the life history of man summed up more briefly and, at the same time, more beautifully, than in that wonderful line? Now follows a companion verse to those just quoted, taken from "Lord of My Heart's Elation," which stands in the forefront of From the Green Book of the Bards. It may be remarked here that while the poet recurs again and again to some favorite thought or idea, it is never in the same words. His expression is always new and fresh, showing how deep and true is his inspiration. Again it is man who is pictured:

A fleet and shadowy column
Of dust and mountain rain,
To walk the earth a moment
And be dissolved again.

But while Mr. Carman's speculations upon life's meaning and the mystery of the future cannot but appeal to the thoughtful-minded, it is as an interpreter of nature that he makes his widest appeal. Bliss Carman, I must say here, and emphatically, is no mere landscape-painter; he never, or scarcely ever, paints a picture of nature for its own sake. He goes beyond the outward aspect of things and interprets or translates for us with less keen senses as only a poet whose feeling for nature is of the deepest and profoundest, who has gone to her whole-heartedly and been taken close to her warm bosom, can do. Is this not evident from these verses from "The Great Return"—originally called "The Pagan's Prayer," and for some inscrutable reason to be found only in the limited Collected Poems, issued in two stately volumes in 1905.

When I have lifted up my heart to thee,
Thou hast ever hearkened and drawn near,
And bowed thy shining face close over me,
Till I could hear thee as the hill-flowers hear.

When I have cried to thee in lonely need,
Being but a child of thine bereft and wrung,
Then all the rivers in the hills gave heed;
And the great hill-winds in thy holy tongue—

That ancient incommunicable speech—
The April stars and autumn sunsets know—
Soothed me and calmed with solace beyond reach
Of human ken, mysterious and low.

Who can read or listen to those moving lines without feeling that Mr. Carman is in very truth a poet of nature—nay, Nature's own poet? But how could he be other when, in "The Breath of the Reed" (From the Green Book of the Bards), he makes the appeal?

Make me thy priest, O Mother,
And prophet of thy mood,
With all the forest wonder
Enraptured and imbued.

As becomes such a poet, and particularly a poet whose birth-month is April, Mr. Carman sings much of the early spring. Again and again he takes up his woodland pipe, and lo! Pan himself and all his train troop joyously before us. Yet the singer's notes for all his singing never become wearied or strident; his airs are ever new and fresh; his latest songs are no less spontaneous and winning than were his first, written how many years ago, while at the same time they have gained in beauty and melody. What heart will not stir to the vibrant music of his immortal "Spring Song," which was originally published in the first Songs from Vagabondia, and the opening verses of which follow?

Make me over, mother April,
When the sap begins to stir!
When thy flowery hand delivers
All the mountain-prisoned rivers,
And thy great heart beats and quivers
To revive the days that were,

Make me over, mother April,
When the sap begins to stir!

Take my dust and all my dreaming,
Count my heart-beats one by one,
Send them where the winters perish;
Then some golden noon recherish
And restore them in the sun,
Flower and scent and dust and dreaming,
With their heart-beats every one!

That poem is sufficient in itself to prove that Bliss Carman has full right and title to be called Spring's own lyrist, though it may be remarked here that not all his spring poems are so unfeignedly joyous. Many of them indeed, have a touch, or more than a touch, of wistfulness, for the poet knows well that sorrow lurks under all joy, deep and well hidden though it may be.

Mr. Carman sings equally finely, though perhaps not so frequently, of summer and the other seasons; but as he has other claims upon our attention, I shall forbear to labor the fact, particularly as the following collection demonstrates it sufficiently. One of those other claims is as a writer of sea poetry. Few poets, it may be said, have pictured the majesty and the mystery, the beauty and the terror of the sea, better than he. His Ballads of Lost Haven is a veritable treasure-house for those whose spirits find kinship in wide expanses of moving waters. One of the best known poems in this volume is "The Gravedigger," which opens thus:

Oh, the shambling sea is a sexton old,
And well his work is done.
With an equal grave for lord and knave,
He buries them every one.

Then hoy and rip, with a rolling hip,
He makes for the nearest shore;
And God, who sent him a thousand ship,
Will send him a thousand more;
But some he'll save for a bleaching grave,
And shoulder them in to shore—
Shoulder them in, shoulder them in,
Shoulder them in to shore.

In "The City of the Sea" (Last Songs from Vagabondia) Mr. Carman speaks of the seabells sounding

The eternal cadence of sea sorrow
For Man's lot and immemorial wrong—
The lost strains that haunt the human dwelling
With the ghost of song.

Elsewhere he speaks of

The great sea, mystic and musical.

And here from another poem is a striking picture:

... the old sea
Seems to whimper and deplore
Mourning like a childless crone
With her sorrow left alone—
The eternal human cry
To the heedless passer-by.

I have said above that Mr. Carman has had three distinct periods, and intimated that the poems in the following collection are of his third period. The first period may be said to be represented by the Low Tide and Behind the Arras volumes, while the second is displayed in the three volumes of Songs from Vagabondia, which he published in association with his friend Richard Hovey. Bliss Carman was from the first too original and individual a poet to be directly influenced by anyone else; but there can be no doubt that his friendship with Hovey helped to turn him from over-preoccupation with mysteries which, for all their greatness, are not for man to solve, to an intenser realisation of the beauty and loveliness of the world about him and of the joys of human fellowship. The result is seen in such poems as "Spring Song," quoted in part above, and his perhaps equally well-known "The Joys of the Road," which appeared in the same volume with that poem, and a few verses from which follow:

Now the joys of the road are chiefly these:
A crimson touch on the hardwood trees;

A vagrant's morning wide and blue,
In early fall, when the wind walks, too;

A shadowy highway cool and brown,
Alluring up and enticing down

From rippled waters and dappled swamp,
From purple glory to scarlet pomp;

The outward eye, the quiet will,
And the striding heart from hill to hill.

Some of the finest of arman's work is contained in his elegiac or memorial poems, in which he commemorates Keats, Shelley, William Blake, Lincoln, Stevenson, and other men for whom he has a kindred feeling, and also friends whom he has loved and lost. Listen to these moving lines from "Non Omnis Moriar," written in memory of Gleeson White, and to be found in Last Songs from Vagabondia:

There is a part of me that knows,
Beneath incertitude and fear,
I shall not perish when I pass
Beyond mortality's frontier;

But greatly having joyed and grieved,
Greatly content, shall hear the sigh

Of the strange wind across the lone
Bright lands of taciturnity.

In patience therefore I await
My friend's unchanged benign regard,—
Some April when I too shall be
Spilt water from a broken shard.

In "The White Gull," written for the centenary of the birth of Shelley in 1892, and included in By the Aurelian Wall, he thus apostrophizes that clear and shining spirit:

O captain of the rebel host,
Lead forth and far!
Thy toiling troopers of the night
Press on the unavailing fight;
The sombre field is not yet lost,
With thee for star.

Thy lips have set the hail and haste
Of clarions free
To bugle down the wintry verge
Of time forever, where the surge
Thunders and trembles on a waste
And open sea.

In "A Seamark," a threnody for Robert Louis Stevenson, which appears in the same volume, the poet hails "R.L.S." (of whose tribe he may be said to be truly one) as

The master of the roving kind,

and goes on:

O all you hearts about the world
In whom the truant gypsy blood,
Under the frost of this pale time,
Sleeps like the daring sap and flood
That dreams of April and reprieve!
You whom the haunted vision drives,
Incredulous of home and ease.
Perfection's lovers all your lives!

You whom the wander-spirit loves
To lead by some forgotten clue
Forever vanishing beyond
Horizon brinks forever new;
Our restless loved adventurer,
On secret orders come to him,
Has slipped his cable, cleared the reef,

And melted on the white sea-rim.

"Perfection's lovers all your lives." Of these, it may be said without qualification, is Bliss Carman himself.

No summary of Mr. Carman's work, however cursory, would be worthy of the name if it omitted mention of his ventures in the realm of Greek myth. From the Book of Myths is made up of work of that sort, every poem in it being full of the beauty of phrase and melody of which Mr. Carman alone has the secret. The finest poems in the book, barring the opening one, "Overlord," are "Daphne," "The Dead Faun," "Hylas," and "At Phædra's Tomb," but I can do no more here than name them, for extracts would fail to reveal their full beauty. And beauty, after all is said, is the first and last thing with Mr. Carman. As he says himself somewhere:

The joy of the hand that hews for beauty
Is the dearest solace under the sun.

And again

The eternal slaves of beauty
Are the masters of the world.

A slave—a happy, willing slave—to beauty is the poet himself, and the world can never repay him for the message of beauty which he has brought it.

Kindred to From the Book of Myths, but much more important, is Sappho: One Hundred Lyrics, one of the most successful of the numerous attempts which have been made to recapture the poems by that high priestess of song which remain to us only in fragments. Mr. Carman, as Charles G. D. Roberts points out in an introduction to the volume, has made no attempt here at translation or paraphrasing; his venture has been "the most perilous and most alluring in the whole field of poetry"—that of imaginative and, at the same time, interpretive construction. Brief quotation again would fail to convey an adequate idea of the exquisiteness of the work, and all I can do, therefore, is to urge all lovers of real poetry to possess themselves of Sappho: One Hundred Lyrics, for it is literally a storehouse of lyric beauty.

I must not fail here to speak of From the Book of Valentines, which contains some lovely things, notably "At the Great Release." This is not only one of the finest of all Mr. Carman's poems, but it is also one of the finest poems of our time. It is a love poem, and no one possessing any real feeling for poetry can read it without experiencing that strange thrill of the spirit which only the highest form of poetry can communicate. "Morning and Evening," "In an Iris Meadow," and "A letter from Lesbos" must be also mentioned. In the last named poem, Sappho is represented as writing to Gorgo, and expresses herself in these moving words:

If the high gods in that triumphant time
Have calendared no day for thee to come
Light-hearted to this doorway as of old,
Unmoved I shall behold their pomps go by—
The painted seasons in their pageantry,
The silvery progressions of the moon,
And all their infinite ardors unsubdued,

Pass with the wind replenishing the earth

Incredulous forever I must live
And, once thy lover, without joy behold,
The gradual uncounted years go by,
Sharing the bitterness of all things made.

Mention must be now made of Songs of the Sea Children, which can be described only as a collection of the sweetest and tenderest love lyrics written in our time—

—the lyric songs
The earthborn children sing,
When wild-wood laughter throngs
The shy bird-throats of spring;
When there's not a joy of the heart
But flies like a flag unfurled,
And the swelling buds bring back
The April of the world.

So perfect and complete are these lyrics that it would be almost sacrilege to quote any of them unless entire. Listen however, to these verses:

The day is lost without thee,
The night has not a star.
Thy going is an empty room
Whose door is left ajar.

Depart: it is the footfall
Of twilight on the hills.
Return: and every rood of ground
Breaks into daffodils.

There are those who will have it that Bliss Carman has been away from Canada so long that he has ceased to be, in a real sense, a Canadian. Such assume rather than know, for a very little study of his work would show them that it is shot through and through with the poet's feeling for the land of his birth. Memories of his childhood and youthful years down by the sea are still fresh in Mr. Carman's mind, and inspire him again and again in his writing. "A Remembrance," at the beginning of the present collection, may be pointed to as a striking instance of this, but proof positive is the volume, Songs from a Northern Garden, for it could have been written only by a Canadian, born and bred, one whose heart and soul thrill to the thought of Canada. I would single out from this volume for special mention as being "Canadian" in the fullest sense "In a Grand Pré Garden," "The Keeper's Silence," "At Home and Abroad," "Killoleet," and "Above the Gaspereau," but have no space to quote from them.

But Mr. Carman is not only a Canadian, he is also a Briton; and evidence of this is his Ode on the Coronation, written on the occasion of the crowning of King Edward VII in 1902. This poem—the very existence of which is hardly known among us—ought to be put in the hands of every child and youth who speaks the English tongue, for no other, I dare maintain—nothing by Kipling, or Newbolt, or any other of our so-called "Imperial singers"—expresses more truly and more movingly the deep feeling of love and reverence which the very thought of England evokes in every son of hers, even though it may never have been his to see her white cliffs rise or to tread her storied ground:

O England, little mother by the sleepless Northern tide,
Having bred so many nations to devotion, trust, and pride,
Very tenderly we turn
With welling hearts that yearn
Still to love you and defend you,—let the sons of men discern
Wherein your right and title, might and majesty, reside.

In concluding this, I greatly fear, lamentably inadequate study, I come to the collection which follows, and which, as intimated above, represents the work of Mr. Carman's latest period. I must say at once that, while I yield to no one in admiration for Low Tide and the other books of that period, or for the work of the second period, as represented by the Songs from Vagabondia volumes, I have no hesitation in declaring that I regard the poet's work of the past few years with even higher admiration. It may not possess the force and vigor of the work which preceded it; but anything seemingly missing in that respect is more than made up for me by increased beauty and clarity of expression. The mysticism—verging, or more than verging, at times on symbolism—which marked his earlier poems, and which hung, as it were, as a veil between them and the reader, has gone, and the poet's thought or theme now lies clearly before us as in a mirror. What—to take a verse from the following pages at random—could be more pellucid, more crystal clear in expression—what indeed, could come closer to that achieving of the impossible at which every real poet must aim—than this from "In Gold Lacquer".

Gold are the great trees overhead,
And gold the leaf-strewn grass,
As though a cloth of gold were spread
To let a seraph pass.
And where the pageant should go by,
Meadow and wood and stream,
The world is all of lacquered gold,
Expectant as a dream.

The poet, happily, has fully recovered from the serious illness which laid him low some two years ago, and which for a time caused his friends and admirers the gravest concern, and so we may look forward hopefully to seeing further volumes of verse come from the press to make certain his name and fame. But if, for any reason, this should not be—which the gods forfend!—Later Poems, I dare affirm, must and will be regarded as the fine flower and crowning achievement of the genius and art of Bliss Carman.

R. H. HATHAWAY.
Toronto, 1921.

Bliss Carman – A Short Biography

William Bliss Carman was born in Fredericton, in New Brunswick on April 15th 1861. 'Bliss' was his mother's maiden name. She was descended from Daniel Bliss of Concord, Massachusetts, who was the great-grandfather to Ralph Waldo Emerson.

Carman was educated at Fredericton Collegiate School. Here, under the influence of the headmaster George Robert Parkin, he gained an appreciation of classical literature and was introduced to the poetry of many of the Pre-Raphaelites especially Dante Gabriel Rossetti and Algernon Charles Swinburne.

From here he graduated to the University of New Brunswick, obtaining his B.A. there in 1881. As is common with so many writers his first published piece was for the University magazine and for Carman that was in 1879.

England now beckoned and he spent a year at Oxford and then the University of Edinburgh (1882–1883). He returned home to Canada to work on his M.A. which he obtained from the University of New Brunswick in 1884.

Tragically his father died in January, 1885, followed by his mother in February of the following year. Carman now enrolled in Harvard University for a year. There he met and was part of a literary circle that included the American poet Richard Hovey, who would become his close friend, and later collaborator, on the successful Vagabondia poetry series. Carman and Hovey were members of the "Visionists" circle along with Herbert Copeland and F. Holland Day, who would later form the Boston publishing firm Copeland & Day and, in turn, launch Vagabondia.

After Harvard Carman briefly returned to Canada, but was back in Boston by February of 1890 saying "Boston is one of the few places where my critical education and tastes could be of any use to me in earning money. New York and London are about the only other places." However, he was unable to find work in Boston but was more successful in New York becoming the literary editor of the semi-religious New York Independent. There he helped Canadian poets get published and introduced them to a wider readership than they could receive in Canada.

However, Carman and work as an editor were not destined for a long career together and he was dismissed in 1892. There followed short stays with Current Literature, Cosmopolitan, The Chap-Book, and The Atlantic Monthly. Whilst these appointments provided the basis for a career and an income he was not suited to their demands. From 1895 he would only work as a contributor to magazines and newspapers whilst he worked on his volumes of poetry.

Carman first published a book of poetry in 1893 with Low Tide on Grand Pré. He had written the title poem in the summer of 1886 and it had (whilst he was still at Harvard) been published in the spring of 1887 by Atlantic Monthly. Despite its critical acceptance there was no Canadian company prepared to publish the volume. When an American company did so it went bankrupt. Life was becoming difficult for the young poet.

The following year was decidedly better. His partnership with Richard Hovey had given birth to Songs of Vagabondia and it was published by their friends at Copeland & Day. It was an immediate success. The young men were delighted at such a reception. It quickly sold out and was re-printed a number of times. Although these re-prints were small (usually 500-1000 copies) they were frequent.

On the back of this success they would write a further three volumes, which in their turn were almost as successful. They quickly became the center of a cult following, especially among students who empathized with the poetry's anti-materialistic themes, its celebration of personal freedom, and its glorification of comradeship."

The success of Songs of Vagabondia prompted the Boston firm, Stone & Kimball, to reissue Low Tide on Grand Pré and to hire Carman as the editor of its literary journal, The Chapbook. This ceased after a year when the company relocated and Carman expressed his desire to remain in Boston.

In 1885 Carman brought out Behind the Arras, a somewhat more serious and philosophical work centered on the premise of a long meditation using the speaker's house and its many rooms as a symbol of life and the choices to be made. However, the idea and its execution did not quite meld.

Signficantly, in 1896, Carman met Mrs Mary Perry King, who rapidly became patron, adviser and sometime lover. She put money in his pocket, and food in his mouth and, when he struck bottom, often repaired his confidence as well as helping to sell the work. She also later became his writing collaborator on two verse dramas.

Mitchell Kennerley, Carman's roommate wrote that, "On the rare occasions they had intimate relations they always advised me of by leaving a bunch of violets — Mary favorite flower — on the pillow of my bed." If her husband, Dr. King, knew of this arrangement he seems not to have objected. He was a great supporter of Carman's career and seemingly his wife's complicated involvement with that.

In 1897 Carman published Ballad of Lost Haven, a collection of poetry about the sea. Its notable poems include the macabre sea shanty, The Gravedigger. The following year, 1898, came By the Aurelian Wall, the title poem itself was an elegy to John Keats and the book a collection of formal elegies.

In 1899 his publisher, Lamson, Wolffe was taken over by the Boston firm of Small, Maynard & Co., who had also acquired the rights to Low Tide on Grand Pré. The copyrights to of his books were now held by one publisher and, in lieu of earnings, Carman took what would ultimately be a disastrous financial stake in the company.

As the century turned Carman was hard at work on what would eventually be a five-volume set of poetry; "Pans Pipes". Pan, the goat-god, was traditionally associated with poetry and the coming together of the earthly and the divine. The five volumes were all published between 1902 – 1905.

The inspiration for this came from Mary who had persuaded Carman to write in both prose and poetry about the ideas of 'unitrinianism.' This drew on the theories of François-Alexandre-Nicolas-Chéri Delsarte and was defined as a strategy of mind-body-spirit harmonization aimed at undoing the physical, psychological, and spiritual damage caused by urban modernity. The definition may be rather woolly but for Carman it resulted in some very fine work across the five-volume series. This shared belief between Mary and Carman created a further bond but did isolate him from his circle of friends.

The excellence of a number of these poems did much to install Carman as the most noted of Canadian Poets and eventually their own Poet Laureate. Among the most often quoted and printed are "The Dead Faun" (from Volume I), "Lord of My Heart's Elation" (Volume II) and many of the erotic poems from Volume III.

In the middle of publication in 1903, Small, Maynard failed and with it went all the assets Carman had tied up in the company.

Carman immediately signed with another Boston publisher, L.C. Page, who would publish seven new books of Carman poetry in this hectic period up to 1905. They released a further three books based on Carman's Transcript columns, and a prose work on Unitrinianism, The Making of Personality, that he'd written with Mary King.

Carman now felt secure enough to pursue his 'dream project,' namely a deluxe edition of his collected poetry to 1903. Page acquired the distribution rights on the condition that the book be sold privately, by subscription. Unfortunately, the demand wasn't there and it failed. Carman was deeply disappointed and lost faith in Page. However, their grip on his copyrights was absolute and sadly no further collected editions were to be published during his lifetime.

By 1904 his income was restricted and the offer to be editor-in-chief of the 10-volume project, The World's Best Poetry, was eagerly accepted.

For Carman perhaps his best years as a poet were now behind him. From 1908 he lived near the Kings' New Canaan, Connecticut, estate, that he named "Sunshine", or in the summer in a cabin in the Catskills, which he called "Moonshine."

With Literary tastes now moving away from what he could provide his income further dwindled and his health started to deteriorate.

In 1912 Carman published the final work in the Vagabondia series. Richard Hovey had died in 1900 and so this last work was purely his. It has a distinct elegiac tone as if remembering the past works themselves.

Although Carman was not politically active he did campaign during the World War One, as a member of the Vigilantes, who supported the American entry into the titanic struggle on the Allied side.

By 1920, Carman was impoverished and recovering from a near-fatal attack of tuberculosis. He returned to Canada and began to undertake a series of publicly successful and somewhat lucrative reading tours, saying "there is nothing worth talking of in book sales compared with reading. Breathless attention, crowded halls, and a strange, profound enthusiasm such as I never guessed could be,' he reported to a friend. 'And good thrifty money too. Think of it! An entirely new life for me, and I am the most surprised person in Canada.'"

On October 28th, 1921 Carman was honored at a dinner held by the newly-formed Canadian Authors' Association, at the Ritz Carlton Hotel in Montreal, where he was crowned Canada's Poet Laureate with a wreath of maple leaves.

Carman is placed among the Confederation Poets, a group that included his cousin, Charles G.D. Roberts, Archibald Lampman, and Duncan Campbell Scott. Carman was perhaps the best and is credited with the widest recognition. However, whilst the others carefully supplemented their income with writing novels and works for the magazines, or even other careers, Carman only wrote poetry together with a small amount of writing on literary ideas, philosophy, and aesthetics.

He continued his reading tours, and by 1925 had finally secured a new Canadian publisher; McClelland & Stewart (Toronto), who issued a collection of selected earlier verse and would now became his main publisher. Although they benefited from Carman's increased popularity and his revered position in

Canadian literature, his former publisher L.C. Page would not relinquish its copyrights to his earlier works.

In his last years, Carman was a member of the Halifax literary and social set, The Song Fishermen and in 1927 he edited The Oxford Book of American Verse.

William Bliss Carman died of a brain hemorrhage, at the age of 68, in New Canaan on the 8th June, 1929. He was cremated in New Canaan and his ashes interred at Forest Hill Cemetery, Fredericton, with a national memorial service held at the Anglican cathedral there.

It was only a quarter of a century later, on May 13th, 1954, that a scarlet maple tree was planted at his graveside, to honour his request in the 1892 poem "The Grave-Tree":

Let me have a scarlet maple
For the grave-tree at my head,
With the quiet sun behind it,
In the years when I am dead.

Bliss Carman – A Concise Bibliography

Poetry Collections
Low Tide on Grand Pre: A Book of Lyrics (1893)
Songs from Vagabondia (1894)
A Seamark: A Threnody for Robert Louis Stevenson (1895)
Behind the Arras: A Book of the Unseen (1895)
More Songs from Vagabondia (1896)
Ballads of Lost Haven: A Book of the Sea (1897)
By the Aurelian Wall: And Other Elegies (1898)
A Winter Holiday (1899)
Last Songs from Vagabondia (1901)
Ballads and Lyrics (1902)
Ode on the Coronation of King Edward (1902)
Pipes of Pan: From the Book of Myths (1902)
Pipes of Pan: From the Green Book of the Bards (1903)
Pipes of Pan: Songs of the Sea Children (1904)
Pipes of Pan: Songs from a Northern Garden (1904)
Pipes of Pan: From the Book of Valentines (1905)
Sappho: One Hundred Lyrics (1904)
Poems (1905)
The Rough Rider: And Other Poems (1909)
A Painter's Holiday, and Other Poems (1911)
Echoes from Vagabondia (1912)
April Airs: A Book of New England Lyrics (1916)
The Man of The Marne: And Other Poems (1918)
The Vengeance of Noel Brassard: A Tale of the Acadian Expulsion (1919)
Far Horizons (1925)

Later Poems (1926)
Sanctuary: Sunshine House Sonnets (1929)
Wild Garden (1929)
Bliss Carman's Poems (1931)

Drama

Bliss Carman & Mary Perry King. Daughters of Dawn: A Lyrical Pageant of a Series of Historical Scenes for Presentation with Music and Dancing (1913)
Bliss Carman & Mary Perry King. Earth Deities: And Other Rhythmic Masques (1914)

Prose Collections

The Kinship of Nature (1904)
The Poetry of Life (1905)
The Friendship of Art (1908)
The Making of Personality (1908)
Talks on Poetry and Life; Being a Series of Five Lectures Delivered Before the University of Toronto, December 1925 (Speech). transcribed by Blanche Hume. 1926.
Bliss Carman's Scrap-Book: A Table of Contents (Pierce, Lorne, editor) (1931)

Editor

The World's Best Poetry (10 volumes) (1904)
The Oxford Book of American Verse (U.S. editor) (1927)
Carman, Bliss; Pierce, Lorne, editors (1935). Our Canadian Literature: Representative Verse, English and French.

www.ingramcontent.com/pod-product-compliance
Lightning Source LLC
Chambersburg PA
CBHW060055050426
42448CB00011B/2471